# Odes to Lithium

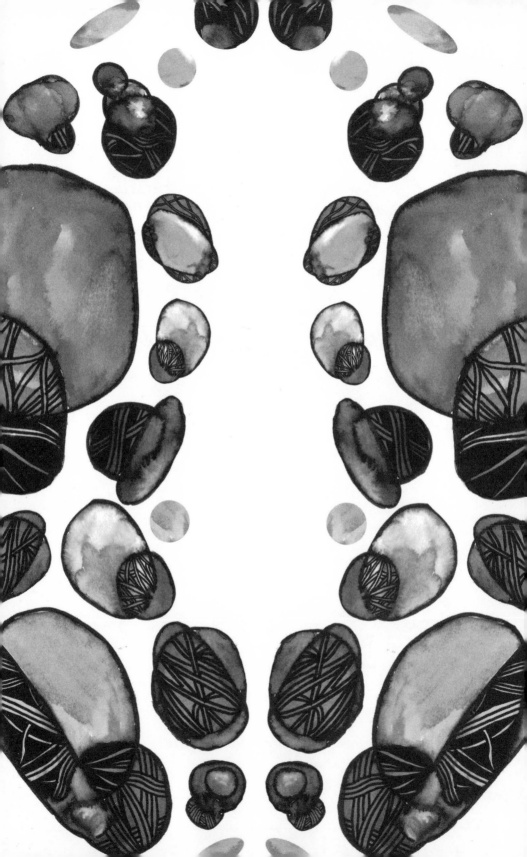

# Odes to Lithium

POEMS BY

SHIRA ERLICHMAN

ALICE JAMES BOOKS
FARMINGTON, MAINE
ALICEJAMESBOOKS.ORG

10 9 8 7 6 5 4 3 2 1

Alice James Books are published by Alice James Poetry Cooperative, Inc.,
an affiliate of the University of Maine at Farmington.

Alice James Books
114 Prescott Street
Farmington, ME 04938
www.alicejamesbooks.org

Library of Congress Cataloging-in-Publication Data

Library of Congress Cataloging-in-Publication Data

Names: Erlichman, Shira, author.
Title: Odes to lithium / Shira Erlichman.
Description: Farmington, Maine : Alice James Books, [2019]
Identifiers: LCCN 2019012543 (print) | LCCN 2019015655 (ebook) | ISBN
9781948579599 (eBook) | ISBN 9781948579032 (pbk. : alk. paper)
Classification: LCC PS3605.R576 (ebook) | LCC PS3605.R576 A6 2019 (print) |
DDC 811/.6--dc23
LC record available at https://lccn.loc.gov/2019012543

Alice James Books gratefully acknowledges support from individual donors, private foundations,
the University of Maine at Farmington, the National Endowment for the Arts, and the Amazon
Literary Partnership.

Cover art: "Peace Mind" by Shira Erlichman
All ink drawings are by the author.

# CONTENTS

## I
### KNIFE-FLOWER

## II
### COCKROACH

## III
### BABY & I

## IV
### THE MONK

To Mom

*In loving memory of my safta*
*Beatrice Claire Aronson Spector*
1929 - 1989

In an extraordinary act of love,
I took control of a celestial star.

—Pablo Neruda, "Ode to a Star"

# I

# KNIFE-FLOWER

# SNAKES IN YOUR ARMS

You are in the neurologist's office for the fifth time in two months. "The tests came back normal," he says. You exhale. On a separate note, you have just spent four days in a psychiatric facility. You had been experiencing symptoms you could only describe as The Edge of Death. So you checked yourself in. You are twenty-five years old and responsible. You are taking medication. You are relieved to hear that your arms, which have been tingling inexplicably for months, check out fine. "It's not your spine," he says. "And it's not your neck. It all came back normal."

Normal.

"OK," you say. Since he is your specialist, and you have trusted him, you say: "I should let you know, since you're my specialist, I was in a psychiatric ward last week. I thought I had Depression, but they say I have Bipolar Disorder. I hear that sometimes inexplicable pain arises with people that have Bipolar. Could that maybe have something to do with my tingling?"

That's when he gets cold. His upper body freezes. He leans half-an-inch back in his blue chair. (He is handsome, only a few years older than you. When you changed into a gown and he saw your unshaved legs, you were embarrassed. In another circumstance, you might want to kiss him.) He has a buzz cut, barely-there stubble, and a degree in pain.

He speaks slowly, with calculation, but there is still a softness there. "Well, what do your arms feel like now?" The young doctor asks.

"It feels—" you pause, you want to get this right, you look for the right word to describe the sensation that has been haunting you, causing you to get test after test, plaguing your sleep. "It's like needles, but they move." How should you describe it? You only have twenty minutes with this man in his office on the other side of the city before you have to go back to Kit's house and sleep on her couch before finding a new place to live before finding a new therapist before deciding how to live tonight, let alone the rest of your life.

"It feels like there are snakes in my arms. Electric snakes that move quickly, like little zaps, through my forearms and wrists." You are a poet and sometimes it helps you and sometimes it distances you from others.

He leans in. Whispers: "Do you really think that there are snakes in your arms?"

You feel tricked. Catch-the-crazy. Whack-a-mole. Burn the witch. You take a full seven seconds before you exhale. In this little white room, where he has hung his certifications up, where his tools to investigate pain gleam on their shelves, and his awards are multiple.

*"Of course not,"* you say.

He visibly relaxes. As if he has done his job.

# SIDE EFFECTS

The side effect of Lithium (is dehydration & peeing more frequently. The side
effect of dehydration & peeing more frequently is not wanting to drink water at all
because you pee more frequently. The side effect of not wanting to is not doing.
The side effect of not doing is a couch & three movies. The side effect of a couch
& three movies is *what have you been doing all day* with a raised eyebrow. The
side effect of a raised eyebrow is a sigh. The side effect of a sigh is plaque. The
side effect of plaque is a dirt road but you're bikeless. The side effect of bikeless is
an unrelenting heartbeat with a passion for waves. The side effect of a passion for
waves is dream upon dream where every object is as blue as the sea. The side effect
of overwhelmingly blue dreams is a girlfriend who listens. The side effect of this
particular girlfriend is black soap that sits staining the side of the tub. The side effect
of stains is her name in your cheek like a cool marble. The side effect of her name
is your hands pulling chicken apart into a big bowl that she is also filling & every
now & then she shakes near your face a ligament so nasty you both squeal & it is
good. The side effect of it is good is it is bad. The side effect of it is bad is crossing
your legs in the psychiatrist's office, talking about side effects. The side effect of side
effects is living your life. The side effect of living your life is dying. The side effect of
dying is being remembered. The side effect of being remembered is being held like
a stone, but of course it is not a stone but a bird that too will die. The side effect of
a stone that is not a stone is throwing the stone & watching it fly. The side effect of
flight) is a poem.

# BEATRICE

My grandmother
is in a red dress &
clapping. My
grandmother,
who never wears
red, is clapping in
my kitchen.
I am pouring
milk into a bowl
of Raisin Bran.
It is a Sunday
morning. Her
grey hair is
in a tight bun
ribboned through
with daffodils.
My grandmother
is buried
in Jerusalem under
pink earth.
*You did it*, she says,
while I spoon cereal
into my mouth.
The linoleum is cold
under my bare feet.
I twist the see-through
orange bottle open, lay
the dose on the counter.
It is the day of rest.
But she has traveled
all these miles
to watch me swallow,
to pull a flower
from her skull &
weave it into mine.

# CLIFF

The Summer I was wrong, or arrogant, or hopeful, I told my Psychiatrist I could be rid of you
by ⅔. In fact, I'd started adjusting the dose myself. *I'm being honest with you*, I told her,
*I feel fine*. When she listened without flinching, when she agreed to swiftly diminish
your touch, her office was rock-still. We were on the 18th floor of a skyscraper.
She was pregnant, her hands folded over new life. You are a graceful
mammoth. You didn't wince, or scream. My baby, I should have
listened. I would have heard your loyalty to my darkest waters.
In the ascending months, & the grey matter of sleeplessness,
I came to know what your absence always means. Cliff.
Every day knived sharper & doused in electricity.

# THEY

I was two days out when Kit threw a small dinner party. A few friends, tough meat, mapled carrots and soon talk turned political. The guest seated directly in front of me said, "I guess I just don't see why they need them."

*They.*
*I guess.*
*Need.*

I didn't throw a chair, identify myself. I didn't educate, or look at Kit. I wouldn't be the one who days earlier wandered electric hallways, or slept in a foreign bed, who vomited the misassigned drugs and sparked with slinking visions. No. I focused my fork on a single pea, threaded the tiny planet, and examined it in the always changing light.

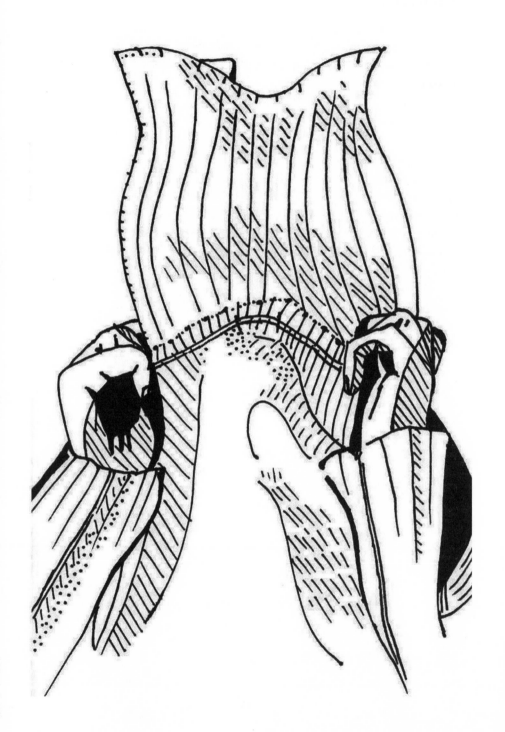

# NEEDLE

"3,        2,        1"
exact as a bully
my dark syrup filling
one vial, two.
I watch the slow reddening,
rendering of human sap.
it's a monthly ritual
to allow a stranger
to collect what is inside me
for assessment:
a shadow of poison,
or clear skies?

here sits a woman
partitioned into numbers
which swell truthfully, kindly—
tiny comprehensions of vastness
charted by a professional
eye

but
even as the nurse counts down,
casts the needle's fishing line, pulls
dawn into delicate vials
I know what the sea knows
with the bottom of its mind
unfathomed

# GHAZAL, INTERRUPTED

Brother, snow-smothered road turned mute
In my doorway. In my nakedness, let me explain.

Father, back turned, makes my bed with me still
In it. "You frighten," but I cut him off let me——

Mother, stomach turning, lifts spoon. I'm not
Sick let   let   prophet I'm     me    explain.

Lover turns the volume up while I cry
So the neighbors think we're dancing.

Doctor turns toward my bloodshot eyes.
I'm certain of all every I've got it just let

# UNREQUITED TEACHER

My hands tremor & a slowness fogs me, my girl
& I just fought, I clean my dish so hard
it flies from my hands & shatters.
You, my infinitesimal gargoyle,
chaperone of my darkness, watch me bend to sweep
the shards into the dustpan
& *laugh*, dare to speak of God (what a word
for a medicine to utter)—of Reason & Presence &
How to Roll with It, Baby. I spit
in your hand, call you ruthless.

  "It's true," you say, "give me enough time
& I'll anvil your kidneys, lose your memory for you."
I tear open lesson after lesson, cursing
each like a hangnail. My little impossible guru.
Prom date to the infinite void. You say: "Don't worry,
everything's out of control." You say:

  "Men become accustomed to poison
by degrees." In all my drama I can't argue
with the master. You kiss me awake & tuck me in.
Instead of *Darling*, you whisper *Mortal*.

# UNWISHED FOR

I'm standing in my town's ice cream shop when I notice them: the white couple smiling at me. Blonde woman standing beside a mailbox, waiting patiently for news, husband reassuringly placing a hand on her shoulder. The flyer they're on is pink: international color of positivity in the face of infertility. They are having a hard time, my couple. That's why they're here in my ice cream shop. But they have faith, they're trying, haven't quit wanting what they want, in spite of it all.

> *Could you be the one?*

I lick the crest of my cone slowly, examine their bullet-pointed criteria.

> *21 to 42 years.*

It's not conscious, but somewhere inside a voice says: "Check."

> *No criminal record.*                          "Check."

> *No history of mental illness.*

I say, out loud to the paper, not caring if the teenager behind me churning into an icy chunk with a steady fist hears, I say: "I know this is different, Susan, Jim, but I would never wish Frida to not have been hit by that trolley. I would never look her in the face and say, 'I choose to unmake you and your paintings and your horror-ing heart. I rob the woods of your little deer.'"

"It's different," Susan says, "you're not Frida."

"Plus," adds Jim, "*that* was physical. A freak accident. Try another argument."

What they don't want of me lives. It sees through my eyes that they would prefer it dead. It knows better than to whimper, or show defeat. What they don't want of me breathes.

"Eugenicists," it says.

The woman gasps, hand to chest.

It continues: "You want to spare yourselves. That's not love."

"We don't want her to suffer," they chime in unison. Oh—*her*? It was decided: A girl. Claire. Or, Vanessa. Or, Claire. She'd have red curls, love olives, sing in her sleep.

"She doesn't want to suffer either," I peel the words open slowly, "but she'd rather be *alive*, than *not suffer*."

I am not talking to a piece of paper in Herrell's Ice Cream Shop. I am not invoking Frida. I am not naming an unloved ghost Claire. I'm licking my wrist of a smudge of strawberry cream, listening to the terrible Top 40 hit blaring overhead. I'm staring at the words *No history of mental illness*, trying to move my feet, and leave the world where this is taped up, natural as the moon.

Will the Norman Rockwell of our time paint me standing here before it? In my jean cutoffs, finishing what's left of a soggy cone, drugs in my blood, unwished for by strangers.

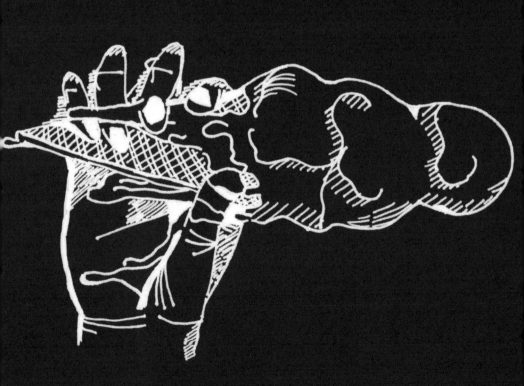

# SIDE EFFECTS II

*memory loss*

I still sing Britney Spears in my birthday suit
pull my hair into a top knot & thread in
fake flowers I copped at the 99 cent store

*tremor*

When she presses down on the accelerator
I catch wind in my teeth, my skull
out the window like a Labrador, speakers popping

*dizziness*

Six rings a hand, neck drizzled in chains
I take myself out, movie ticket for one, pull
Twizzlers two-by-two from sticky plastic

*increased thirst*

The fresh basil I toss on my sunny-side up
plus a sweating glass of spiced iced tea
swirling is a spell, air heavy with light

*vertigo*

I paint my mouth pink & cat-eye my lids
before heading out into the rain
with a twenty in my chest pocket

*coma,*
      *blurred vision,*
              *startled response,*
*blackout spells   tinnitus   hallucinations*
*tics  taste distortion   worsening*
*of organic brain syndrome   dry mouth*

*fatigue fever hyperirritability salty taste*
*swollen lips tightness in chest eventual*
*blindness incontinence hyperthyroidism*
I make a plan for tomorrow, I make a plan
for tomorrow, I make a plan for tomorrow

run the shower hotter
roll the frozen globe of a grape
from roof to cheek
Little God that I
am

# THE KNIFE-FLOWER

I fell all over myself that year. Reading Neruda
between Linguistics and Statistics,
leaning on a cool hallway wall near the ROTC
while just ahead soldiers practiced their marching.
I drank a steady chalice of ode after ode after ode.
Second year of college, second semester,
somebody stop me. Lust was my terrain. I licked
my plate clean. Underlined what was already
underlined. My religion, those muscular, inky odes.
The beloved class, *Neruda in Translation*.
For our Final: a loose assignment
the Art Majors loved. My classmate,
a Bio Major (satisfying some remote credit)
constructed out of clay a lily
whose stem sharpened into a green knife.
Collision of images from a Neruda poem.
She painted it so intricately, from a distance
it looked real. At the end of class I weighed it
in my palms, tiny death-life, precious contradiction,
my baby. "Take it," she said, without ceremony.
And just like that,
it was mine.
Days later my father picked me up
for Spring Break. We lay the gentle knife-flower in the back seat.
If he had been more tender, he would have buckled it in.
But when we arrived and he lifted it from its cradle,
it split in half. Immediately my mouth formed "It's okay,"
even though the break looked dooming.
Embarrassed at the lengths he'd taken,
and how the gift had broken anyway,
he voiced a soft apology, fumbling the two pieces in his hands.
Took the pieces into his back office
with the small pirate ship and the drawing of fifty cats
I'd made for his fiftieth birthday
and quietly glued knife to flower.
When he gave it back to me, the gift was heavier.

But look, that room:
him hunched over the ruins, owl-glasses on,
the once-engineer threading a secret silk
through the fractures because he'd promised me
something akin to wholeness.

# NATURAL

*Each subway car will be left on the ocean floor, to be assimilated into the*
*ecosystem. Over time, every surface will be covered in life, creating an*
*artificial coral reef.*

> —"Stunning Photos Showing NYC Subway Cars Being Dumped into
> the Ocean," *Viral Forest*

Today I don't want to take you
so I imagine you a subway car
push you        over my edge
to rust at my seafloor.
Ferment & flower, metallic

traveler. I've been thrown
off my axis            so-
rrow's my monogamous
love. Once I shunned you
wanting to be "natural"—

tea tree milk, sprouted
cashews, bark deodorant
"natural." Stopped taking you
& soon was lost in snow
stroking branches for hours for

hours walked jagged     circles
muttering sudden secrets revealed
by ice                    wept.
Against my will I swallow two
busted down caterpillars

let you        sink to the bottom.
"It's not personal," I tell myself.
Even the sea needs        even
the sea            needs, the sea
needs, even the sea

# II

# COCKROACH

# I'M SITTING WITH BJÖRK IN MY BATHTUB

& she leans, takes my knee in her mouth, like a puppy.
this is her song. I am a pale mountain from her native
landscape. she moans & it is my name. it is not sexy, it is
sexual. my blue wrist suckled in her other mouth is an
enchilada. I think about how my car won't sell on
Craigslist. I think about how ill-prepared I am to do my
taxes. she can tell my mind is elsewhere. she doesn't
mind. she sucks a peach. I take her photograph & it is a
Selfie. there are so many ways to need yourself. a faint
nipple through the bubbles. she has no reason to hide
from me. we are sisters in the army of almost. it is the
way we flirt. we are never bored. Björk uses a can-
opener to open the bathwater. it's working.

she slides my mental hospital evaluation papers into the
water, so they dissipate into tiny paper fish. this is her
song. I am a mossy stone remembering its past life as a
bird. she names every doctor who never met my eye. it is
not political, it is a curse. my chest is an ivy wall
replenished by her hacking hands. I think about how I
threw up the bad medicine. I think about being told to
*just swallow it.* she can tell I am reliving the neon isolation
of mind-jail. she doesn't flinch. just sucks a jawbreaker. I
see her tongue change color & exhale a fuck of rivers.
there are so many ways to crown yourself. a perfect
nipple glaciers thru. she has no reason to judge me. we
are sisters in the queendom of Self. it is the way we work.
we are sweetened sweat. Björk puts a straw to my
forehead & drinks the suds. it's lovely. her eyes are truth
wagons chugging along ancient dirt.

# DEAR DR. STONE

Doctor at the Trauma Unit at McLean Hospital,
or at least when I met you, you were.
I say your name because I can't believe it is your name.
How appropriate. You who called me out of my small room
in the mental hospital,
off my bed where I sat stunned,
having just arrived in the unblinking light of 7 a.m.
having slept on a gurney in the ER.
You stared straight through my skull
like there was a movie on behind me
and listed medications to it.
*You deserve your name.*
I remember thinking that.
Looking into the prophecy of your face
and seeing a hard substance,
center of a drupaceous fruit, as in a peach.
Stone, also a verb, to throw stones at,
to kill by throwing stones.
You listed "Trihexyphenidyl" and I said, "I've taken that."
You said, "Seroquel and Risperdal." I remember
I even tried to like you, starting with the mole on your chin.
I thought, *If I can like that small brown stone,*
*I can like her.*
Your lips were tight, your chin barely bobbed,
your eyes committed to the plot of abyss through and behind me,
but I tried, because even on the worst of all mornings,
I wanted to trust something, even if it was you.
Wanted your name to foretell a polishing.
In the electric glaze of a mania-maze I felt
a smooth baby shark swimming in my cerebellum
and I kept saying,
"I've taken that."
You landed on "Abilify." I said,
"That one made me throw up, it made me sick."
Monotone, you instructed,
"You're going to take it again."

Through the slap of neon lights, to a face unmoving:
"But I took it, it made me puke."
You wrote the prescription.
Maybe you were a mother. It was possible.
Maybe you were dead. There are ways
to be both. Maybe you once became a doctor to heal
an unhealable fissure in your quiet and flaming past,
or because you were curious, passionate, even
kind. Now here I was, one of many puzzlebodies
come to sit in your windowless room, rickety proof
of a faulty universe, a Godless God,
girl who couldn't or wouldn't be solved.
There is a calculus to apathy.
I retreated to my small room to sleep
two days on a wiry bed frame on public sheets
that had belonged to others' private sweat.
On the first day I swallowed your prescription
and collaged a paper-mache journal.
On the second day I vomited
the Abilify on the carpet.
When I returned to your office,
you checked some boxes,
made no eye contact,
said, "Well, now we know."

# THERE WERE OTHERS

I have to be honest with you: there were others.
      & some of them were good. Before you gilded my hippocampus
I lay in bed with fireworks: antipsychotics, their distant cousins,
      Risperdal, Abilify, all the dizziest bees.

When the SSRIs asked me to dance, I danced, heavier than I've ever been,
      a weeping clockwork, but at least in motion.
Some even pinched a smile from me. I know you want to know:
      Were they better Did I love them Would I ever go back Who was she.

But if you could see what they gave me: years.
      From the bottom of the lake they scraped my literacy for breathing.
Or: my mother & I, side by side on a king-size bed, reading
      while they ambled & flit through my thick helplessness.

      I read books. I cooked meals. Forgive me.

# MARGOT

We're at camp, skipping archery.
The cabin is dark, poorly sewn curtains
left loose. Margot has silky brown hair
to my tangles, breasts to my not yet.
On the top bunk, my head in her lap,
she cups my chin, draws a mustache
beneath my bottom lip, says,
"Talk." I sing, going the extra mile.
Her face, also two faces. Lying
in her lap, the world flips rightside down.
It doesn't matter if she'll love me back.
We're getting away with something.

# THE TWO THINGS I REMEMBER FROM FRESHMAN PHYSICS CLASS

1. Ms. Kissel's deep love for her cockroaches.
2. Relativity.

I'll start with Ms. Kissel: barely 5'2'' with a red-headed pixie cut. It is her second year teaching public high school and it shows. The whole year Roc, a tall, freckled, hell-on-legs, calls her by her first name and only raises his hand to make fart noises. Quaking Ms. Kissel, bargaining with Roc to "Please, stop?" while he pops his gum, snorts. Then there is Crazy Willy, perpetually clad in black with floppy, unwashed hair. He was just Willy before The Incident, which should be a solid foreshadowing for you.

One day Willy raises his hand and when called upon staples his middle finger. The class goes silent. Ms. Kissel shrieks, which is what any human being would do. But we are high schoolers, forever fronting. To us her reactivity is ludicrous, a delicious edge, our tiny teacher's face stretched beyond recognition in terror. Poor Ms. Kissel, begging Crazy Willy to go to the Nurse while he just smiles, bug-eyed, no one's child.

But the one time we all give her our undivided attention is after Thanksgiving. "How was your break?" she asks, and before we can answer she interrupts, begins describing a three-hour car ride to her parents' place for the holiday and how she took her pet cockroaches with her in the back seat because "no one could take care of them." Now we are riveted, and she is tall with story, her arms windmilling describing all six roaches freezing to death on the ride over because her heat was broken. How she wept all the way home, speeding, hands choking the wheel.

We are teenagers, judgemental, freakishly un-ourselves, but we are listening. We think we know how this goes. Some of us throw out a few real condolences, until Ms. Kissel twists to face Willy, her eyes glowing, her smile bucking. "When I got to my parents' house I put the little fish tank in front of the fireplace. I waited. Ten minutes passed. And then, one by one, their little legs began to twitch." Someone in the back throws a fist into the air. Another stops chewing her pencil to gasp. "They lived."

It's true. But what I remember most about the story is that she cried. As if her heart longed to kiss the vermin awake. No disgust. Lithium, my despicable stranger, you too have a hard shell, your own flawless antennae. Every morning and every night I swallow your bitterness, the imposed disgrace, the so-called proof of a shortcoming or defect or lack. Say what you will about roaches, what she loved would not die.

# MIND OVER MATTER

I tried. But mind over matter is a joke. The mind
is matter. Someone's unprofessional opinion
was to "relax" over matter. To sandcastle over
wave. They aimed to clean up a murder scene
from behind a plate of glass. It was my murder.
Mine. As if I could possess the firegrief that
possessed me. Wrestle the wind to the floor for
daring enter my house. But it's just me down
there, gripping my shoulders, threatening my
own heart. Have you ever seen the dark split
into two peaches? Sickness is a lot like that.
To the uninitiated it looks like fruit. Wise, shiny,
certifiably cherry. Do you mind if I die while I
say it? Rot that my teeth met: *my fault*. Would it
matter if I tried while I died? Will you relax
the coffin into the soil? If you don't have blood
on your hands by the end of this you weren't
listening.

# THIRTEEN WAYS OF LOOKING AT PHINEAS GAGE

Phineas is on my back porch, rod through his head, smoking a cigarette. Handsome as the day he was struck. Bolt of congealed lightning, left eye closed up, dark hair soft on his open skull.

•

The sun is setting so I slug back my metallic pellets, feeling foolishly aligned with him. "I've done my research on you," I flirt, "Phineas: Greek for *mouth of brass*." He shrugs, "Guess so," talks around the metal splitting the roof of his mouth.

•

We're old friends. Kissed once to test the waters, but found we liked talking and fighting better. Still, we lie in bed. It's time to flip the record. In the static he drags a slow thumb across my forehead, "You've got your own pole," he says like a fortune-teller, "two of them. High and low. Get it?" I don't like clever men, but his hand lingers on my forehead, blessing.

•

He's trying to take it out himself. Stands in the bathroom, pulls. The mammoth splinter won't budge. Shirt off, he glares at the mirror. I lean against the doorway, "I thought the rod blew clean through you, landed eighty feet away." He turns toward me slowly, a sternness in his jaw when he says, "But you *do* see it?" It nearly grazes the ceiling. I can't look anywhere else.

•

"When it happened to you, what did your friends say?" he asks, hand still on my forehead. I shift uncomfortably under his one eye. "Some brought me gifts: a scarf, a pomegranate, get well soon cards. Some disappeared altogether." Phineas bends closer, "No. What did they say *about you*?" Instantly, as if a seashell were put to my ear, I hear the tangled choir of his friends discussing him: "Fitful." "Irreverent." "Changed."

•

I need a night out, so I leave him on the couch where he's been crashing. He marveled at the microwave for a full hour before he curled up in a blanket to eat ready-made mashed potatoes. I find Geoffrey, Brette, Anne, and Ma at the back table of the bar, already buzzed. They know about Phineas, and after the third round they don't hesitate to pry. No, we haven't fucked. Yes, he's funny and strange and kind. No, we don't need a doctor. Yes, he's real. No, he's not real. Brette grabs me by the wrist, her gaze intimate with booze, "How does it end?" My phone buzzes, Phineas wondering how to work the washing machine, though he has nothing to wash.

•

"Again," I beg.

*"Doctor, here is business enough for you."*

"No, the whole thing!"

"Alright. It was late afternoon. I was working on the railroad when the iron sparked against the rock and the powder exploded. The iron rocketed through my face, behind my eye, out of my head and landed eighty feet away, smeared with blood and brains. They say I convulsed, then got up, walked to the oxcart, rode all the way to the house, and when I saw him, said...'Doctor, here is business enough for you.'"

We can't stop laughing. He starts to get up from the bed, but I grip his shoulders. "Again."

•

We study him in school. In the black and white photograph, he grips the iron, half-smiling, looks the way he does at my kitchen table at 3 a.m. pouring another bowl of cereal. The textbook is heavy. He's four whole pages of it. "The standard when it comes to brain injuries," says my professor. The class chatters: was he never the same? A brute? Or was he, as some wrote, a miracle? No one says "both."

•

The only time he's allowed out is onto the back porch to smoke. We both agree this is for the best. Can't have the neighbors calling 911. "You're a constant emergency," I

36

joke. He takes a drag, assesses the darkness.

•

My mother drops by unannounced. Phineas strains spaghetti over the kitchen sink. She stumbles backwards, can't tear her eyes from the silver saber impossiblizing itself through his head. On the phone a week later she says to me, "You were always such a serious child. At ten, you couldn't sleep. Then, with everything that happened to you, I suppose I always knew something like him would come." I want to correct her, "*Someone* like him," but I don't. I catch sight of him behind the cracked bedroom door, changing his shirt, the shadow of him two shadows, blood caked to the back of his neck.

•

When it happens, it isn't final. I'm not his. He won't necessarily stay. He covers me like a weed, eats my earlobe, fast hands climbing me, strains to slow down. The entire time the bottom of the javelin nearly slices my throat. But he's careful, knows how to maneuver the harpoon. When we kiss I taste metal. "More," I say. He thinks I mean him. I mean me. If it weren't for the specter of shrapnel suspended above me, this would be normal. Besides that, it is. The fan spins. A dog barks. His hipbone is his hipbone.

•

I want to live like my neighbors: splashing olive oil on a pan, slicing fruit into fun squares. Phineas won't get in the shower. It stings to be alive. Mid-conversation he's suddenly beyond me, lost to a place I can't go. At the table he mindlessly pours pepper. "You're not here *or* there," I complain. He tells me that when he dreams it's about the railroad, simple tasks he never finished. One hundred and fifty years have passed and still he wants to lay down tracks, steel a road into place.

•

One night I say, "Fuck it," pack him into the front seat, unroll the moonroof for his head. Back road bound, car slippery and bucking through dark swaths of night, I glance over. In flickering slides of streetlight, he is clean-cut and grinning, but most of all, he's robbed of the weapon. Then it's back. Or is it a shadow? Then gone. Back again. It's dizzying so I keep my eyes on the road. He puts his feet on the dash, rolls the window down and up. "Let's get pizza," he teases. It's 1 a.m. and I know Joe's will be packed. He turns the volume up so loud I can't hear my own thoughts, as if to press me further into *yes* and *now*. We fly down roads and then, we're stepping out of the car. Phineas is already ahead of me, crunching gravel. Under the glare of overhead lights we're suddenly surrounded by voices, dough and beer in the air. A teenager raises his eyes from the cash register, his throat caught on hello.

# PORTRAIT OF A RELEASE

It was my mother who picked me up
from the mental hospital—but only to drop me off
at Kit's. Kit is the type of friend who will not only
let you stay at her house after you've been in a mental hospital,
no questions asked, but will give you her bed
instead of the couch. The car ride was silent.
My mother didn't dare speak.
I stared out the window, boiling and frozen.
There was no radio and autumn was Jackson Pollocking
all over our windshield.
The ride from McLean Hospital to Kit's doorstep
was forty-five minutes of foliage and breath.
I remember when she dropped me off at the curb,
my backpack full of clothes, wondering
how she could just drive off.
As if a car, if you were a mother dropping off your child,
should just stop working, dry of gas or brakes cut,
forcing mothering to take effect.
But I got out, said a one-syllable goodbye,
and the car pulled away with my mother inside.


•


Four days is a long time in a mental hospital.
How do you even fill one day in a mental hospital?
Where do you go? Who do you talk to?
When the pay phone rang and some sleepy body shouted for me,
I asked if it was my parents, and if it was,
I wouldn't answer.
The one time I did answer, my mother spoke
like a garden hose full of holes, spouting everywhere,
"I'm sorry, I'm sorry, it should have been different."
And the sad thing is, the garden hose was trying,
it was actually elegant in its miserable mess,
it was trying.
But the thing about "I'm sorry"

when you're hearing it from a phone booth
in a neon hallway of a mental hospital, is that it doesn't really
mow your lawn, it doesn't really cut your steak, you know?

•

Four days of avoiding the girl who wanted to tell me
why she didn't really belong in this ward.
Four days of collaging paper-mache to a journal
and banging a stupid tiny drum in "Music Therapy."
Four days of knowing your parents are paying
the hospital bill and wondering if they resent you.
Four days of irreconcilable boredom,
which gives way to awe at the glory of autumn
outside your barred window.
Four days of reading Rumi by yourself in your room.
Four days of bathrooms without locks.
Four days of nurses with minuscule paper cups
of experimental doses.
Four days in which "I'm sorry" is like a bird
thrashing against your window.

•

Kit's house is a twenty-minute walk
from Faulkner Hospital, where I'll be an Outpatient,
which basically just means I don't sleep there.
For a week and a half, for six hours a day, I am
a body in a chair listening and talking
with other bodies in chairs. I don't cry.
Not for myself. At least, not here.
But I do cry for others whose stories undo my sense
of capital J Justice. In all their stories
there is a common thread: someone didn't listen.
Sometimes it is a brother, or a wife,
sometimes it is a mother.

•

On my morning walks to the hospital
I am shellacked in beauty. Red leaves falter
like prayer flags on the branch. Yellow leaves grin
their good yellow teeth. When I start to think of my family,
my father stewing somewhere in evergreen sweatpants
and a private, heavy rage, or my brother
ignoring his feelings, moving like a bolt of brunette lightning
through his days, or most vividly, my mother,
guilt eating her heart like a silkworm on the vine,
I practice a Cognitive Behavioral Exercise
the Group Therapist taught us.
It's simple and it works:
notice the colors around you.
In ROYGBIV order.
This will reroute your brain
away from the emotional center, where mother happens,
toward the logical center, where math happens.


•


Red: leaves, stoplight,
jacket on a woman down the path,
red fleck of paint on my brown boots.
Orange is how headlights look when they're turned off midday;
where are these cars going? To work? To family?
Orange is a tree shaking its arms like a bad dancer.
Orange is the sign advertising a new TV show,
one lost orange glove near the bus stop bench.
Yellow, slutty tree,
oh cerebellum, oh Lithium,
do your job.
Oh cortex, oh frontal lobe, throw me into a logic
that doesn't make me think of family.
Yellow nails, yellow-pale cloud
in an otherwise blue sky.
Green trees losing to autumn,
green grass with signs: *Keep Off.*
Green jacket on a man walking toward me.

Blue sky. Blue sky. Blue jacket on me.
Blue car. Blue building with white trim.
Indigo, what is indigo anyway?
Violet's moody sister. Purple, let's just say,
and it's nowhere.
A car, dark purple, that'll do.
A passing woman's cold lips.
The hospital is not purple. If it was,
it wouldn't be a hospital. It wouldn't be
a serious place. Purple is a flower color
and color, all color, is something my mother loves.

# SOMEONE ELSE'S MOTHER

Helena Joy drank pickle juice from the jar, stole
my green nail polish, egged on her humping rabbits, killed
the basement light so I couldn't find my hands, cracked
too many eggs into the batter, enjoyed the hatch & fester
of a lie in her mouth, named every doll after herself, tore
fake bills out of my fists & claimed the game, carefully laid
three drawings on the rug: legs, torso, face of some man
& ground her hips against him. In her dusty Victorian
with nibbled chalk in the driveway & a circular pool in the back,
she chewed her long braid & poured syrup. When maggots galloped
from the bottle's lip onto our pancakes, her body chose
a laugh. But unlike her, I couldn't leave them, or, they wouldn't
leave me. Later, I climbed the ladder & edged the lip of the
pool, plastic blue tarp sealing it for autumn, & fell in, writhing
in my sudden coffin. My useless hands grasped no rail until
it was her mother, three hundred pounds lifting me,
having heard the splash from the living room & run fast,
fastest to me, my own mother behind her.

# ROSE

a friend says

*but*
*you*
*don't*
*seem*
*like*
*you*
*have*
*Bipolar*

mouth kind, whole as a bell, mouth
I care for, whose shoelaces I'd tie &
cup I'd fill

do you know what it's like
to want to believe a non-believer?

suddenly I am
undiagnosed
another girl
a cloud
made rabbit
by a child

surely
you know how this ends

a rose
by any other name
is still a flock
of blades

# AFTERTASTE

I wash you down
with thick milk I bought today
from a farmer with skin made orange-grey
from the handling of ancient dirt
whose eyes crinkle at their pretty corners when I drop
my change into his palm, old pennies new dimes flickering
nickels, uncorroded bright weight
of metal slipped easy as a dog's kiss
lapped up in the hand

It's true:
everything
on this brutal blue
dot is constructed of elemental attraction
& I wash you down with a tall glass of the whitest white
wash you down, soak the salt of your body in my salt,
thinking, sweetly actually, of the side effect
*metallic aftertaste*

I know, right now, in a distant laboratory you
are being mixed with aluminum, copper,
manganese, cadmium to make
planes strong yet featherweight
they need you
because you are famous
for being the lightest
of your cousins

It's because of you

something heavy should fly

# III
## BABY & I

# DAVEEN

Blonde, chipper, & with a name like a cleaning solution
the young nurse catches my drool in a mini paper cup
as I spit out the meds, again. This is her third try. She sighs.
Only a few years older, Daveen grabs me under-the-armpits,
transports me to the chair, then wheels me to the room
at the hospital's end. Someone/a stranger/everyone
is disappointed in me. Ten days later I'm *released*—is what
they call it. She breaks strict code to walk me through
the heavy doors to my car in the lot, lightly punches my shoulder
like a stepsister. I'm not just outside, I keep thinking, I'm Out.
With nothing to gain, Daveen pulls me in close. She's hugging me
so tight, spots choke my vision. With all this concrete fog
in my head it's hard to hold on to a sentence but she says
"I hope," she says "I never," says "see you," says "again."

# THE TIGER

*Every single tiger is special. Each one has feelings, thoughts, and dreams.*
*These tigers are not here by chance. They came to me looking for protection.*
—Monk, Wat Pa Luangta Bua monastery, Thailand


I call you Lithium in one fell swoop erasing your idiosyncratic taste. The one that clung to the roof of my mouth as if arguing with the path ahead. The one who bubbled in my empty gut, admonishing me like a mother for missing a meal.

I should call you Lithiums. The one whose skull came dented, I pondered for a full five seconds. The one Siamese-twinned to his brother, who with a fingernail I surgeoned.

In my dream you came back as tigers. I roamed through your bodies, salted orange. You had faces, sometimes kicked in sleep, twitching toward a kill. But when I moved through your forms, swishing the sea of your backs, you never harmed me. But you were never tigers. You were the one who prefered to bathe in the morning, the one who prefered to bathe at night.

When I wake up there's just an orange bottle, you lie still inside, though it's no cemetery. I pour the day's family into my palm.

After thirty days, when it's empty, there's always the same scene. Escaped powder lines the bottom of the bottle. I lick my pinky. I eat your thoughts.

# LIGHTWEIGHT

at the party I'm called a *lightweight*

while you shovel salt through my blood
like a dedicated father clearing the driveway

except the driveway is the whole world

you make wine take off its clothes faster
glaze my eyes with gentle & I deserve a life-

time supply of this ease    so when they

tease "just one drink & you're *good*"
they don't know        it's not the wine

somebody cares for me

# IN THE HANDS OF

I sit down but before she
throws the smock around my neck
to take up the issue of my hair,
to douse in hot-hot spray & comb fingers through,
at times too rough, working the untangling,
to douse again in heat, the nozzle's mouth grinning
a centimeter from my scalp,
before she says, "How much off?"
I say, "It's been a hard couple months. Can you
be gentle with me." Too late. Already naked
in the apple orchard, the other students working
their way around me. Or that sleepless Fall
on his voicemail: *They're trying to kill
me.* Our parents, of course. (Should I tell her
bangs? Just a trim?) Or a hospital bed hijacked
by demons, I wet; years later the thought that
someone had to clean it. (Take it all off.)
"A hard couple months" means I thought
my father killed children, touched them, me.
"Be gentle" means you can't, but.

# ON THIS END

I.

Love Mom                      communicate with me          find some way to

I hope that you will      my predicament      consider my feelings and

please               I ask you to          a lost child

I have a missing or         I feel like         deeply

and care about you        because I love        is excruciatingly painful

this disconnection        what to do or say      I struggle with

except your silence        no information      since I have        to no avail

respectfully and gently         out unobtrusively      to reach

genuine efforts        of this I have made       the outcome

but wonder      I can't help      and months have passed      very clear

you have made your feelings      of me        who is part

from my daughter        disconnect      in complete      life

I can't live my         unbearable      more        it's

with each day        to respect your request       done my best

I have        is taking its toll on me      you have asked for

this space and time      I am writing you this note because      Dear Shira.

II.

Love Shira        on this end        to no avail        to me is not

     you reaching out      it feels like it      I understand

also while     for us to speak     getting to be about time     that it is

     begin healing I agree     have needed months to just     so painful that I

   to my illness and self      responses      the family's

of this past Fall were so terrible and       the events       for me

  heartbreaking      which would be      estrangement

       the outcome be     I have never intended that

on my own     and firm footing     to gain safety     I have needed

 towards this      who I am in order to move     to be seen for

 as well as     in my family     relationships all around     healed

the outcome I want is     you deeply and     I love and care about

this weekend     we can check in     you have given me     time

  the space and     I appreciate     are suffering     I understand you

are packed with work     tomorrow Thursday and Friday     on the weekend

  if not then     on Friday evening     this week most likely

      you     I will call     Hi Mom.

# THE WATCHMAN

How this, sparkler in the night's black field, lighting up my brain
with love How did they do it before you—survive Your elegance
of salt, rock, & sleep, who invented How can such a small watchman
keep safe all my hills & homes Why pink, your face—not cobalt,

green, or just white Who thought you deserved your delicate hue
What do my organs think of your soft arrival each day Who unlocks
the door to let you in, like a wet cat How did you lift the heaviest
season from my eyelids, sweeping away a whole cloud How do you

pollinate my blood so exactly with sanity Does my brain's infinite
heart burden you Why find my grandmother too late
Why not kiss everyone who needs your fix Why leave some
to their singed waves Who do you speak to in my body that listens

# POSTSCRIPT TO MANIA

It's not easy dying every second
for the sake of some mission.
What-the-Fuck-ologist, leading me
by the softest whim toward the blade.
Chicken wire undulated behind my lids
& the sky looked beat to death.
I've been going through my files. Who
was that? At what precise moment
did my brain tattle on itself? Everything
was a wick. Even God was worn down
by my false sirening. It's not easy dying
without dying. Before I ever took the pills
I took so much. So much was taken. I'm
done. I'm here. A fish thrown back
to the river can't help but swallow fistfuls
of self.

# A SERIOUS CASE

In liquid form, you scared me. It was a fellow Outpatient, black bangs pasted to sweaty forehead, sliced up arms & shoulders, teeth pointy as a rat's, who introduced us. She opened her vial in the hospital cafeteria just as I was setting down my tray at her table. Slurped you casually from her finger, her dripped-down wrist.

"Yum," she said, locking eyes with me. Or did she? Did she cackle? Did she moan? I remember a smile teeming like wormed-through soil. A girl from *The Craft*, that kind of witch, back-of-the-class cutter, a serious case with a Big League prescription.

Sure, just weeks ago I'd roamed my college campus naked, cooing to neon ghosts, till I found myself immobile, pissing a hospital's bedsheets in totalitarian fear. But I wasn't *her*. I picked up my tray, moved to another table. She kept licking her fingers, which was your way of calling after me.

# BABY & I

"Baby, come help me."

"Honey, pass me a flathead."

Greg the Plumber has been here before, replaced a radiator, hit on me.
Today he's flanked by Nick & Paco, or, Baby & Honey.
Nick, a six foot dude in dirty elbows & his mid-twenties & a wolf-beard
oafs over to Greg, who strokes a clanging vent in my bedroom.
In & out the hallway Honey begins the group task of carrying large pieces
of sink out my front door: glimmering white bones of former infrastructure.
Everyone is busy, but Nick finds me in the kitchen:

> "I saw your book in there. You got Bipolar too?"

It's so like me, to leave private thoughts loudly on my bed. "Yes."

> "I take meds & everything. Zyprexa & Seroquel. You?"

When I say Lithium it is a fact, like telling him what city I was born in
& finding out he's from there too. Baby grins.
When he laughs, he claps his hands together like he just
came in from the cold. He could not be my brother, but he is
my darling. I want to slice a peach for him, or at least fetch a glass
of water so I do but as soon as I love him he is gone.

Years ago, I would've said,        "Nope."

But there's a wolf grinning in my bathroom, Baby,
taking everything out—piece by piece—but the air.

# CONVERSATION WITH K.

friend I rarely see / bowl of coffee between us / daffodils shaking
out of concrete / lone / pigeon circling / our ankles / for scraps / he

    told me of sleeplessness / the fucking / maxed-out credit cards / entire
    family at rope's end / cheated-on girlfriend more worried than mad

the Ecstasy / the drinking / the Ecstasy / punctuating the conversation
"But I don't want to take medicine" / spoke of God / not wanting to

    change who he was / all roads I'd sown / but stable now / for years / thriving
    even / I listened / thinking I knew something / blunt / told him what I took

saw his eyes simultaneously flicker yes & distance / I outlined
his hand / titled each finger / with what might need attention / sleep / food /

    tactic / I'd learned in group / & books / just months ago I'd made
    the choice: down on my dose to a barely / traceable amount / felt

healthy enough to try / but was still fiercely protective / of you
defended you / listed all your gifts / secrets / knowing you'd want me to

    knowing you lived / to serve / I sat tall with facts / while he closed
    door after door in your face / still / I'd call him open

inside the outline / of his wide palm / we sketched options
me I guess / in the position of storyteller / sage / decade of hospital stays

    doses / living-through-it / I thought I knew something / later his friends
    thanked me / family thanked me / he'd made an appointment / was

thinking about you / (tho ultimately would opt against) / what did they know / what did
any of us / know / me especially / me / just weeks later / side of the tracks / screaming

    at a freight train / in the sharpened air / mindmouth / unable to
    stop weeping / inconceivable speeds / no sleep / pushed a ghost

back with my palm / told it to get the fuck / away / the train screaming
back / I should have told him / this is how it happens: how it shouldn't

# PERFECT

*...I needed to do something about my moods. It quickly came down to a choice between seeing a psychiatrist or buying a horse...and since I had an absolute belief that I should be able to handle my own problems, I naturally bought a horse.*
—Kay Redfield Jamison, *An Unquiet Mind*

I didn't seek the horse. Didn't put out an advertisement. They say it can smell you from sixty miles away, which means if I'm in Toledo & the horse ain't she can smell black tea & more than a dollop of shame. The way that one famous octopus could predict the winner of the World Cup by putting a particular ball in a particular basket, that's how much my horse loves me. Nine out of ten times. & by love I mean nearly destroys me for the sake of her own path. She's yellow-eyed & insolent, my Perfect. I didn't name her, she came that way. Her coat is Van Gogh's *Starry Night*, oil on canvas, postimpressionist, you know the one because you've seen a tote bag. What most don't know is it depicts the view from the east-facing window of his asylum room. What most don't know is he added an idealized village. Only the villagers know why. Perfect is the kind of bitch-horse to remind you *Starry Night*'s moon is not astronomically correct. I ride until she's raw & the moon chips a nail on the dark. I ride until my breaths tie 0-0. Paul. That was the octopus's name. May we all deserve such simplicity & too many hands. On Wikipedia you can find Paul's entire life story from his egg hatching in England to present-day affairs. But find me manic & you can't find me. I'm a knobless door. I cook meals for the dead & they eat. I ride the casket like a car, step into traffic like a car but I'm a body. No body can look both ways simultaneously. Except me. I'm an eighteen-layer lust-cake. I prefer Perfect to my own mother, begging. I prefer Perfect's confetti plaque, raining & raining. I ride until her jaw breaks off. It's a type of singing. Fire follows me around like a pet sister. I should be able to handle my own problems is something my mouth once said to my brain. If my funeral hatches soon you can bet it will be well-attended by horses. Muscular, mudslick, expertise sluts. Bucking, exquisite, & murderous. Perfect is a terrorist disguised as a horse. I prefer choosing terror to a terror I didn't choose.

# THE RUNNER

Days after I won the Statewide 6th Grade
Cross-Country Race I was gifted
my first black eye. Two older girls chose *me*
from the whole prepubescent crowd
to follow out of McDonald's to
the phone booths, drench in Sprite,
punch & chase down the open street
laughing

When that fist opened my eye
my feet instinctively paddled,
I ran. Just like you, blazing through me
all push & push, as if you too are being
chased by fools but are more legs
than prayer, claiming breaths
like rungs, memorizing their faces,
but never looking back. I ran like that
covered in my own blood, forgiving
everyone

# POTION

Our first kiss wasn't behind the high school. Not in the movie theater's back row. Not
after the first breakdown. It went like this: me, released from the hospitaljail with
a fresh prescription, one bag packed, staying at a friend's house, with no exit plan
or exist plan. Walking the length of a concrete road, I turned & asked: "Has it been
cloudy for days—& the sun just came out?" She said: "No. It's been sunny all week."
So then. It was your sudden mouth. Your broom that swept the sky of its minor
chord. There's no metaphor here. When I looked up, I saw the sun.

# IF YOU WERE SOMEONE

If you were a man, I'd prefer your Tuesday Schmuck
to your Sunday Best. How enchanting to be bored
together. The results are in: you'd be a good one.
Tongue never sluggish. Busy sautéing the greens.
You'd be organized, measured—no one would know
how incandescent your fucking.

& don't let me conjure the possibility
of a woman: discarded pantyhose haunting my pillow
like a snakeskin. & I taste you & I taste your salt.
You're curt, drink your calendar neat,
eat everything with a pocketknife, don't ask me how.
In motion you're the northern lights, I'm not trying
to get it down with a camera. I tell you *it's over*
& you don't change. I tell you *I need you*
& you don't change. Never a hiss, no one's name
spat. I'm tested, then I hold your hand while we sleep.
You drool.

Or, if you were somewhere in between, either/or,
maybe neither: you'd sit like an anchor at the foot of my bed,
little lighthouse of they, rubbing my feet.
Pour cereal in a bowl before I even ask, drench it
in chocolate milk. Your hands a flash of glow-in-the-dark
nail polish. Your beard a brunch.
You'd flip me & pin, teeth to the back of my neck,
the Prince in your hips flashing. Not myth, not
Minotaur.

   Don't you see?

    At night I shake tablets into my palm.
    But if you were *someone*?
    You'd be real. I'd hold you & thank you.

# CHLOE

*All my family call me Chloe.*
    —Toni Morrison

Turns out, the Nobel Prize-winning author answers to a different name
than the one on the cover. The way God might answer to Sweetheart.
I like to think that when Toni accepts the prestigious award, Chloe
is looking out the window at the jasmine. If Toni acts, Chloe dreams.
Marilyn Monroe slips off her pumps to become Norma Jean.
& isn't this the most sacred division?

What do you prefer?

Carbonate, Citrate, Orotate, or Atomic Number 3?
Mineral? Fascist?
The Tears of Tunupa, Salar de Uyuni,
the World's Largest Mirror?
Dangerous? Dream?
Thank you, No, Never, or Please?

I capitalize your name, though the world says
that's unnecessary——you're an element after all,
no proper noun. But why not, when you're equal
to the women I come from, or our countries?
Capital B Beth, Capital P Poland.
Still, you wear your lowercase happily,
unbothered by being Unpatented
Freak. You never hesitate."Give me a run-on
of epithets & elegance," you dare.

*Lunaticmenschmaniactonic*

You answer You
answer You answer
You answer

# IV
## THE MONK

# 89 LINES ON A BRUISE

The Former Poet Laureate of the United States
    wrote an eighty-nine line poem about clouds & I

want to write about clouds but all I can see
    is this bruise on the inside of my inner-elbow the needle left

when posing a question about my toxicity level.
    One review calls the book "mesmeric...cryptic...profound"

& my bruise could be described as such but who has time
    or stomach for it, indeed as the poet said, "Words about clouds

are clouds themselves" & I for one agree. Meanwhile someone smushed a honeybee
    in three squelches in my elbow crook while a blueberry vein trickles

in the background—could that count as a line about clouds?
    I want so badly a day, nay a minute, devoted to capital N Nature

while she tousles her hair free of sparrows & suggests mountain-y cleavage
    but the bruise is a diva of seventeen costume changes:

Alice Walker purple, underbelly-of-log green, dried-vomit yellow.
    You don't make this easy, cloud.

My bruise returns to chat no matter how hard I try to leave
    illness out of this, which is what's been suggested after all

by gatekeepers: *But why so many poems about it?* You know
    what they say, "Words about bruises are bruises themselves."

The poet writes in lovely, often playful snippets
    I easily & delightfully comprehend

while my dribble of islands hide the radial, brachial, median
    nerve after secret nerve as if to say we walk already buried.

Not a cloud on this body, but a dollop of queasy green, unreadable
     map, trail of disfigured kisses.

I'm alive with jokes the needle told & a nurse so overworked
     I consoled her while she plunged.

Today I rest my fingers on the keys
     brimming with lust to see the sky change.

I'm sorry, sky, this little puddle
     steals my eyes & all eighty-nine lines.

Line 1 is about the purples

Line 2, the greens

3-10. crush of melon

11-16. blue before it hits the light

17. the nurse's small talk

18. if she counts up or down

19. the snap of gloves

20-42. skillful quiet or quiet skill (sometimes it's hard to tell)

43. the waiting room overflowing at 10 a.m. on a Wednesday

44-60. I'm held captive by a vial filling with me

61. flesh mood-rings into another color

62-72. strangers who notice

73. family who doesn't

74-81. lover avoiding the spot with her mouth

82. the results of the toxicity test

83-87. the psychiatrist's voice delivering the news

88. press down

89. the tenderness

# EXCUSE

We've been silent for almost a week now. A hand shoots up.

    *Excuse me I'm mentally ill Excuse me*

"How do I handle my rage in the grocery store line?" Another

    *Excuse me I'm mentally ill Excuse*

can barely get the words out, "My daughter...drug addict...won't let me

    *Excuse me I'm mentally ill*

help...I can't let go." All hands are met. The teacher sits in a spotlight

    *Excuse me I'm mentally*

in the darkened hall in soft robes. I don't raise my hand, but my body

    *Excuse me I'm*

is all hands. Every single sweating palm is layered over my mouth in a

    *Excuse me*

tectonic smothering. I can feel my voice at the core, too hot to

    *Excuse*

reveal

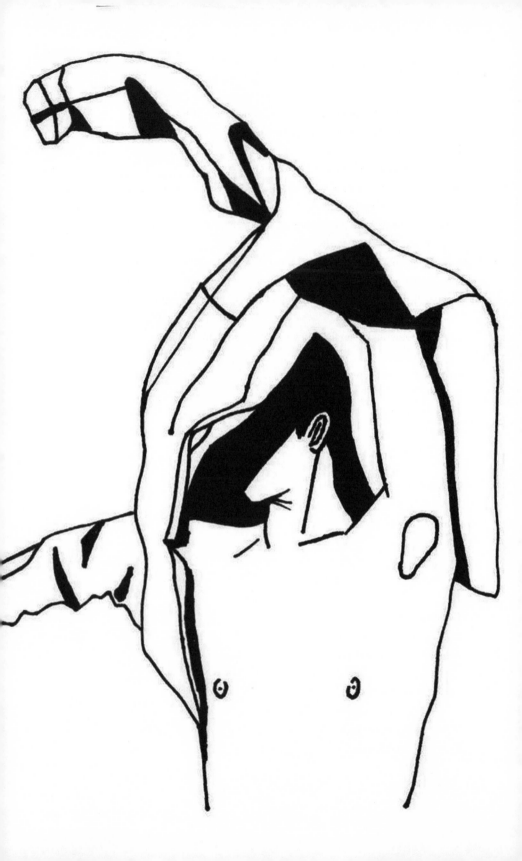

# BAROMETER

I face the ~~hospital~~ bathroom mirror.
My bathroom. My mirror.

I buy too-expensive sunflowers
and let him ~~in on The Plan~~ keep the change.

I grow ~~distant gone unreachable~~ frustrated
with my mother on the phone
and call the feeling *cherishing*.

I ~~die~~ flip the pancake.

I run ~~to the next town~~ the bath.

Give ~~up~~ directions.

I don't know exactly what happened to me.
Who put me here with a mud full of mouth,
cool jar of flowering suns, black bread seething on my table.

My name still serves me. I turn around, say
"pass the ketchup," "thanks but no thanks,"
"~~empty~~ good morning."

~~Once twice three~~ four times
my mind Alka-Seltzered in a cup of abyss.

But look, ~~nothing~~ :
my key's click in the lock.
A bird beyond each window.

I deserve to ~~soar~~ fail.

What I'm trying to say is
Mom, mix my chai.

Angel, parachute the sheet, make our bed our bed.

Hello, mewy stray at my ankle, keep it.

Waiter, afternoon for one. I ~~can't~~ desire.


~~can't.~~


I.

# HOW THE JELLYFISH PROSPERED

It's August in New York
& my lover's alarm
siphons me into the kitchen
as the room fills with clouds.
I don't mind poetry, not even here,
telling you I forgot the glass bottle in the freezer
of all places, shards I'll have to pickaxe
with a butter knife.
*How did I—when?*
There is no question like the body.
I collect its fragments. My little butter knife /
chip / chip / chips. Angel folds her arms
around me while I sift through blue freezer light.

Somewhere far beyond
jellyfish bob on a wave while I gather shrapnel.
My teeth chatter.
Tears polyp at the sudden thought,
*Thanks to this double-edged salt,*
*by the time I'm fifty, will I remember*
*anything at all?*
The butter knife speaks: yield.
Yield.
Who needs memories when you have
arms around your waist?
I wed each wave
as it hits me.

# PINK NOISE

*/ the sound when one puts a shell to one's ear / blood music*

in a recent study, Spanish & Japanese speakers couldn't remember
the agents of accidental events as easily as English speakers could.
why? in Spanish & Japanese the agent of causality is dropped, as in:
"the vase broke itself," rather than "John broke the vase."

/

soft target: a military term referring to "a person or thing that is
relatively unprotected or vulnerable, especially to terrorist attack."

/

in "If I Was Your Girlfriend," Prince sings, "Would u let me dress u /...
Would u run 2 me if somebody hurt u / Even if that somebody was me?"
my brain always sings along to that part: "Even if that somebody was me?"

/

over her third cup of coffee & only minutes after her birth control story
a friend tells me, "No offense but personally I could never take drugs."

/

everyone seems to be lowering their voices these days.
even the pharmacist at the pickup counter whispered, "The *lithium*?"

/

last night in an unprecedented turn of events
I held my suffering to my ear & heard.

/

the brain broke itself
the brain broke itself

        rather than

I broke the brain
I broke the
I broke
I

   /

my illness wants me to note the many meanings of patient:

   1. from the Latin *patiens*, literally: I am suffering
      see also: I endure; allow; submit
   2. constancy in effort
   3. "a minor form of despair, disguised as virtue."
   4. another name for Solitaire, a card game (for one person)
   5. able & willing to bear
   6. calmly or without complaint
   7. an individual awaiting or under [medical] care
   8. the one who is a waiting
   9. the one who is acted upon
   10. the one who is the recipient of
   11. steadfast despite opposition, difficulty, or adversity
   12. steadfast, despite
   13. even if [patient] self-refers as "I," patient is always the; a; one; recipient; solitary

   /

card game (for one person):

   — breakfast is barred windows
   — lunch is a patient who kisses you
   — dinner is wet beef
   — there are no plants
   — a stranger wakes you by asking if you "wouldn't mind"

— a needle in your arm
— "could you answer some questions"
— The Best Facility in the Country

/

card game (for one person):

— mouth moving ninety-nine miles per hour deal a no big deal
every time someone suggests you "might not be a prophet" or
that a nonstop forever has passed glued together only by your
lack of coherence "can you hear me" cohere me "slow down"

/

card game (for one person):

— when dealt the sea, remember
"The sea they think they hear. Singing. A roar. The blood is it."
— when dealt the sea, remember
"Our saints do not differentiate between a disease & a miracle."
— when dealt the sea, remember
"Oceanic other, sounded out, outs itself as inside noise"

/

(disintegrated) card game (for one person):

— I argued with the rain today

/

card game (for the disintegrated):

— I forged my own signature

/

"typical soft targets are places of worship"

/

the brain broke

I hold a shell

/

I'm ill

what they hear:

I'm ill

egitimate

/

I broke the


I

/

rain broke itself

I argued

/

the place of worship

targeted

the place of worship

/

can a terrorist be a

soft target be

a terrorist

/

card game (for one person):

    — on the last day of your hospitalization you wait for mom
    — in the dining area, a soap opera is on TV
    — no one else is in the room
    — while you wait the woman on the screen locks herself in the closet
    — because voices told her to
    — you turn off the TV
    — the screen just a screen now
    — your mother, your mother
    — you leave unconvinced you are leaving

/

after her third cup of coffee & only minutes after her birth control story
a friend tells me, "You're so *brave*."

brave: "a minor form of despair, disguised as virtue."

/

brave: girl in a girl in a girl: nest doll of secret selves
brave: cloud in a vase in the distance: nest doll of no one
brave: *now* in a *must* in a *now*: nest doll of how

/

the name for the shortcut humans make through shrubbery
that becomes preferred to the gravel road is 'desire path.'
without blueprint, we beat our path into the ground
until others can walk there.

/

"What's your dose?" the new psychiatrist asks.
dose, from Greek *dosis*, meaning gift.

/

after a show an audience member says to me, "I just
wanted to introduce myself, I'm one of us."

# THE MONK

I was fifteen when the famous photograph confronted me.
I stood by my boombox, *Rage Against the Machine*
new in my hand, and took it in. The monk sat
in meditative quiet while flames ate
his robe, his being. I didn't know what Buddhism was,
my tongue had never formed the words "self-immolation."
I was just in love with Tom Morello's shriek-bends,
that sledgehammer deviance, the questions his guitar
refused to answer. The album was my gateway
to everything anti-.
In Spanish class I'd slip my headphones on
under my hoodie and wash myself in "Killing in the Name"
while Señor Davíd explained verb usage.
But that night in my bedroom,
studying the photo,
the only word on my mind was *how*.
How was it possible.
How did he just sit there.
And what did that say about me, wincing
when I fell at soccer practice, or too nauseous to blink
every time my period rolled around?
The internet said he did it for capital P Peace,
torched himself so all could benefit.
I cannot help but think of you:
dying into my blood each morning, each night.
What a blessing, my monk,
to be your fire.

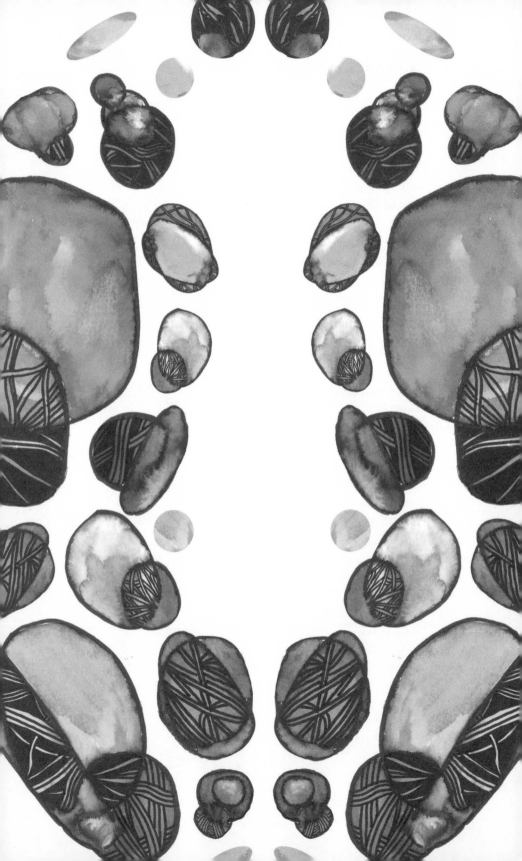

# NOTES

"Unrequited Teacher": the line "Men become accustomed to poison by degrees" is attributed to Victor Hugo.

"Thirteen Ways of Looking at Phineas Gage": Phineas Gage (b. 1823) is neuroscience's most prominent brain-injury survivor. A railroad crew foreman who suffered an accident with a tamping iron, his case was the first to indicate a correlation between brain trauma and personality change.

"The Tiger": the monk quoted appears in the film *The Tiger and the Monk.*

"Chloe": The epigraph from Toni Morrison appeared in a 1994 interview in *The New York Times Magazine.*

"89 Lines on a Bruise": the quote "Words about clouds are clouds themselves" is from *89 Clouds* by Mark Strand.

"Pink Noise": the first stanza cites research by scientist Lera Boroditsky.

"Pink Noise": the quote "[Patience – ] A minor form of despair, disguised as virtue" is from *The Unabridged Devil's Dictionary* by Ambrose Bierce.

"Pink Noise": the quote "The sea they think they hear. Singing. A roar. The blood is it" is from *Ulysses* by James Joyce.

"Pink Noise": the quote "Our saints do not differentiate between a disease & a miracle" is from *I am always searching for something dark & holy to overcome me* by Purvi Shah.

"Pink Noise": the quote "Oceanic other, sounded out, outs itself as inside noise" is by Stefan Helmreich and appeared in *Cabinet Magazine*.

# ACKNOWLEDGMENTS

My gratitude to the editors of the following publications in which these poems, sometimes in earlier versions, first appeared:

*Apogee:* "Postscript to Mania"
*The Baffler:* "Perfect"
*BOAAT:* "Mind over Matter"
*BuzzFeed Reader:* "Snakes in Your Arms"
*Brooklyn Poets* and *Psychology Tomorrow:* "Side Effects"
*Huffington Post* and *The Adroit Journal:* "The Watchman"
*NAILED:* "The Tiger," "Unrequited Teacher, "Lightweight," "Someone Else's Mother" (formerly "The Runner II")
*The Offing:* "Potion"
*PBS NewsHour Poetry Series:* "Natural"
*Perigee:* "Conversation with K." "Excuse"
*Prelude:* "Barometer," "Needle," "A Serious Case," "Beatrice," "Aftertaste"
*Psychology Tomorrow:* "Cliff," "There Were Others," "Side Effects"
*Washington Square Review:* "Margot," "They," "Side Effects II"
*Winter Tangerine:* "I'm Sitting with Björk in My Bathtub"
*Women's Studies Quarterly:* "Ghazal, Interrupted"

For any work of art to move from impulse to realization there has to be a wild confluence, or constellation, of kindnesses. This book-object is proof of these intersecting kindnesses. That the strong net woven for me be fully honored in two small syllables seems impossible. Still, thank you. This cherished net includes you too now, reader.

Thank you to the following residencies for your transformative support: Vermont Studio Center, The Millay Colony for the Arts, and AIR Serenbe. My innermost gratitude to the entire Alice James team, especially Carey Salerno, for believing in this work.

My friends and inspirations, your very being is art—your shoulder touches, bad jokes, and unshatterable spirits. Every day I'm thankful for you. Adam Falkner. Alessandra Genovese. Anna Barsan. Anna Bowers. April Ranger. Aracelis Girmay and Family. Ashley Cassandra Ford. Carlos Andrés Gómez. Casey Rocheteau. Charif Shanahan. Cory Cochrane. Cristin O'Keefe Aptowicz. Dalya Nafis. Danez Smith. Dul Nafis. Elana Bell. Eleanor Kriseman. Eloisa Amezcua. Emily Dix Thomas. Ethan Lipsitz. Eric Hnatow. Eve L. Ewing. Fatimah Asghar. Franny Choi. Giovanna Fischer. H. Melt. Haley Morgan. Hanif Abdurraqib. Hieu Minh Nguyen. Jamila Woods. Jeff Kass. Jeremy Radin. Jessie Levandov. Jozie Furchgott Sourdiffe. The Kagan Trenchards. Karen Smyte. Kaveh Akbar. Kelly Stacey. Kevin Coval. Kit Wallach. Lauren Whitehead. Mahogany L. Browne. Maria Walsh. Marie-Helene Bertino. Marlee Grace. Molly Raynor. Nate Marshall. Ocean Vuong. Paul Tran. Peter Bienkowski. Raymond Antrobus. Saeed Jones. Safia Elhillo. Sara Brickman. Sarah Kay. Ted Dodson. Tommy Pico.

Thank you, Allegra Williams, for the giant snowflake you hung from my childhood bedroom ceiling, the blank music paper you mailed me so I might make sense of the changes in my life, the creative ways you consistently showed up at my door during my most impossible season. You once wrote, "Thank you for having the courage to live inside the hope you wish for [and the courage to] bring us to the edge of fullness time and time again." This remains my compass.

Thank you, Jaime Lowe, Jeanann Verlee, Rachel McKibbens, and Tara Hardy for writing mental illness with such precision and fire. Your risks and contributions are meaningful beyond measure. To my friends, and also to my students, whose writings on mental health nourish and inform mine: Aden Neumeister, Andrea Gibson, Caitlin Shih, Mary Lambert, Morgan Parker, sam sax, and Zaphra Stupple— your truths, and the nuance with which you render them, stitch an atmosphere of freedom.

I'm indebted to the work of Gloria E. Anzaldúa, whose warning, "Wild tongues can't be tamed, they can only be cut out," guides me. To the writers whose words I've used as doors and windows: Audre Lorde, Pablo Neruda, Rumi, and Wisława Szymborska.

My lifelong gratitude and love to Claudia Kaplan and Cassandra Reid. To all of the mental health practitioners who provide safety in chaos. The nameless ER hospital staff who in our brief minutes together told me I "would get through it," played tic-tac-toe with me, or fought to get me the last open room in a packed hospital. To the wise folks of the Northampton Depression and Bipolar Support Alliance (and my mother for suggesting I sit and talk with my people).

To the elementary and high school teachers whose impact is so profound it continues to unfold: Mary Sodano and Abby Erdmann. To mama-guru Patricia Smith for blazing the trail with craft, jewel, and cackle.

Thank you to the spaces that have nourished me: Books Are Magic, Cantab Lounge, the Communion dinner table, Greenlight Bookstore, Insight Meditation Society, SWS, Urban Word, and the Whitehaus Family. Thank you to the In Real Life and Lyrics to Go workshops and the Neutral Zone community.

Thank you to my extended family of cousins, aunts, and uncles. My grandparents, rest in flowers. My ancestors, I follow as you flow through me.

To my precious family, Mom, Aba, and Shai—your love is the salt of the earth. I love you.

Angel, there aren't enough words or hours. Your love has transformed my life. I love this uproarious, honest place called Us. Too, it bears saying, these poems owe your eyes big kisses. Thank you for your tenderness and gravity with them and with me. I, you.

To the creative force that originates all phenomena—whenever I feel awe, I feel you.

Mom, who this book is dedicated to: thank you for the cards in the mail, prayers, advocacy, insistence against shame, allyship, unconditionality, boundaries, persistence, respect, listening, and (from day one) building me a library. Thank you, in short, forever, for you.

Finally, to the mentally ill. This book is most especially, undoubtedly, and gratefully for you. May we keep speaking ourselves into the room until the whole world is our room.

# RECENT TITLES FROM ALICE JAMES BOOKS

*Here All Night*, Jill McDonough
*To the Wren: Collected & New Poems*, Jane Mead
*Angel Bones*, Ilyse Kusnetz
*Monsters I Have Been*, Kenji C. Liu
*Soft Science*, Franny Choi
*Bicycle in a Ransacked City: An Elegy*, Andrés Cerpa
*Anaphora*, Kevin Goodan
*Ghost, like a Place*, Iain Haley Pollock
*Isako Isako*, Mia Ayumi Malhotra
*Of Marriage*, Nicole Cooley
*The English Boat*, Donald Revell
*We, the Almighty Fires*, Anna Rose Welch
*DiVida*, Monica A. Hand
*pray me stay eager*, Ellen Doré Watson
*Some Say the Lark*, Jennifer Chang
*Calling a Wolf a Wolf*, Kaveh Akbar
*We're On: A June Jordan Reader*, Edited by Christoph Keller and Jan Heller Levi
*Daylily Called It a Dangerous Moment*, Alessandra Lynch
*Surgical Wing*, Kristin Robertson
*The Blessing of Dark Water*, Elizabeth Lyons
*Reaper*, Jill McDonough
*Madwoman*, Shara McCallum
*Contradictions in the Design*, Matthew Olzmann
*House of Water*, Matthew Nienow
*World of Made and Unmade*, Jane Mead
*Driving without a License*, Janine Joseph
*The Big Book of Exit Strategies*, Jamaal May
*play dead*, francine j. harris
*Thief in the Interior*, Phillip B. Williams
*Second Empire*, Richie Hofmann
*Drought-Adapted Vine*, Donald Revell
*Refuge/es*, Michael Broek
*O'Nights*, Cecily Parks
*Yearling*, Lo Kwa Mei-en

Alice James Books is committed to publishing books that matter. The press was founded in 1973 in Boston, Massachusetts as a cooperative, wherein authors performed the day-to-day undertakings of the press. This element remains present today, as authors who publish with the press are invited to collaborate closely in the publication process of their work. AJB remains committed to its founders' original feminist mission, while expanding upon the scope to include all voices and poets who might otherwise go unheard. In keeping with its efforts to build equity and increase inclusivity in publishing and the literary arts, AJB seeks out poets whose writing possesses the range, depth, and ability to cultivate empathy in our world and to dynamically push against silence. The press was named for Alice James, sister to William and Henry, whose extraordinary gift for writing went unrecognized during her lifetime.


Designed by Tiani Kennedy
Printed by McNaughton & Gunn